EMMANUEL JOSEPH

The Algorithm of Ambition, A Journey Through Career, Family, and Divine Purpose

Copyright © 2025 by Emmanuel Joseph

All rights reserved. No part of this publication may be reproduced, stored or transmitted in any form or by any means, electronic, mechanical, photocopying, recording, scanning, or otherwise without written permission from the publisher. It is illegal to copy this book, post it to a website, or distribute it by any other means without permission.

First edition

This book was professionally typeset on Reedsy.
Find out more at reedsy.com

Contents

1	Chapter 1: The Spark of Ambition	1
2	Chapter 2: Defining Success	3
3	Chapter 3: Career Climb	5
4	Chapter 4: The Balancing Act	7
5	Chapter 5: Family Foundations	9
6	Chapter 6: Personal Growth	11
7	Chapter 7: The Role of Community	13
8	Chapter 8: Embracing Challenges	15
9	Chapter 9: The Power of Purpose	17
10	Chapter 10: Navigating Transitions	19
11	Chapter 11: Divine Purpose	21
12	Chapter 12: The Journey Continues	23
13	Chapter 13: Mentorship and Guidance	25
14	Chapter 14: Innovation and Creativity	27
15	Chapter 15: Financial Independence	29
16	Chapter 16: Legacy and Impact	31
17	Chapter 17: Reflecting and Celebrating	33

1

Chapter 1: The Spark of Ambition

From a young age, the seeds of ambition are often sown deep within us. It can be sparked by the simplest of experiences—a book that resonates with the soul, a mentor who offers a glimpse of potential, or an inner drive that whispers of greatness waiting to be unleashed. This chapter delves into the origins of ambition, exploring how our childhood dreams and aspirations shape the path we eventually tread. By examining the influence of family, culture, and early experiences, we begin to understand the complexities that fuel our desire to achieve and make a difference in the world.

As we grow older, the spark of ambition can either be nurtured or extinguished. Supportive environments and positive reinforcement play a pivotal role in whether we continue to chase our dreams or abandon them for more pragmatic pursuits. It's essential to recognize the importance of cultivating a mindset that embraces challenge and growth, even in the face of adversity. In this chapter, we'll explore the significance of resilience and determination in keeping the flame of ambition alive.

The journey of ambition is not linear; it is marked by twists and turns, highs and lows. At times, the path may seem clear, while at other times, it may be shrouded in uncertainty. However, it is often during these moments of doubt and confusion that we discover the true essence of our ambition. By embracing the unknown and trusting in our abilities, we can navigate the complexities of our journey with grace and purpose.

Ultimately, the spark of ambition is a powerful force that drives us to push beyond our limits and strive for greatness. It is a testament to the human spirit's resilience and capacity for growth. In this chapter, we will celebrate the beauty of ambition and the unique journeys that each of us embark upon in pursuit of our dreams.

2

Chapter 2: Defining Success

Success is a multifaceted concept that can be defined in countless ways. For some, it may mean reaching the pinnacle of their career, while for others, it may be about finding fulfillment in personal relationships or achieving a sense of inner peace. This chapter explores the various dimensions of success and how our perceptions of it evolve over time. By examining the influences of society, culture, and personal values, we can gain a deeper understanding of what success means to each of us.

In today's fast-paced world, success is often equated with material wealth and social status. However, this narrow definition can lead to feelings of inadequacy and dissatisfaction. It is essential to recognize that true success is not solely determined by external measures, but also by our internal sense of fulfillment and happiness. By redefining success on our own terms, we can create a life that is meaningful and aligned with our values.

One of the key aspects of defining success is understanding the role of failure in our journey. Failure is an inevitable part of the human experience and serves as a valuable teacher. By embracing failure and learning from our mistakes, we can build resilience and develop a growth mindset. This chapter delves into the importance of reframing failure as an opportunity for growth and self-improvement, rather than a setback.

Ultimately, defining success is a deeply personal and evolving process. It requires introspection, self-awareness, and a willingness to challenge societal norms. By embracing our unique definitions of success, we can lead more fulfilling and purposeful lives. In this chapter, we celebrate the diverse ways in which success can be achieved and the importance of staying true to ourselves on our journey.

3

Chapter 3: Career Climb

The pursuit of a successful career is often a central focus of ambition. From choosing the right profession to climbing the corporate ladder, the journey is fraught with challenges and opportunities. This chapter explores the various stages of career development, offering insights into how to navigate the complexities of the professional world. By examining the importance of networking, mentorship, and continuous learning, we can unlock the doors to career advancement and fulfillment.

In the early stages of our careers, it is essential to build a strong foundation. This involves acquiring the necessary skills and knowledge, as well as developing a professional network. By seeking out mentors and building relationships with industry peers, we can gain valuable insights and support. This chapter delves into the importance of mentorship and the role it plays in guiding us through the various stages of our career.

As we progress in our careers, the focus shifts to achieving career growth and advancement. This often involves taking on new challenges, stepping out of our comfort zones, and continuously seeking opportunities for learning and development. By embracing a growth mindset and staying open to new experiences, we can navigate the complexities of the professional world with confidence and resilience.

The pursuit of a successful career is not without its sacrifices. It often requires a delicate balance between professional aspirations and personal commitments. This chapter explores the importance of work-life balance and the strategies for maintaining a healthy equilibrium. By prioritizing self-care and setting boundaries, we can achieve long-term career success without compromising our well-being.

4

Chapter 4: The Balancing Act

Balancing career, family, and personal aspirations is a delicate dance that requires careful planning and flexibility. This chapter delves into the challenges of managing multiple roles and responsibilities, offering practical strategies for achieving harmony. By examining the importance of time management, setting priorities, and embracing flexibility, we can create a life that is balanced and fulfilling.

One of the key aspects of achieving balance is effective time management. This involves setting clear goals, prioritizing tasks, and creating a schedule that allows for both professional and personal commitments. By staying organized and focused, we can make the most of our time and avoid feeling overwhelmed. This chapter offers practical tips for managing time effectively and staying on top of our responsibilities.

In addition to time management, setting priorities is essential for achieving balance. This involves identifying what is most important to us and making decisions that align with our values and goals. By being intentional about how we allocate our time and energy, we can ensure that we are making progress in both our professional and personal lives. This chapter explores the importance of setting priorities and offers strategies for staying true to our values.

Flexibility is another crucial element of the balancing act. Life is unpredictable, and unexpected challenges can arise at any time. By embracing flexibility and being willing to adapt, we can navigate the ups and downs with grace. This chapter delves into the importance of staying open to change and being resilient in the face of adversity.

Ultimately, achieving balance is an ongoing process that requires constant attention and adjustment. It is about finding harmony in the midst of chaos and creating a life that is aligned with our values and goals. In this chapter, we celebrate the beauty of balance and the unique ways in which we can achieve it.

5

Chapter 5: Family Foundations

Family is the cornerstone of our lives, providing love, support, and a sense of belonging. This chapter explores the importance of family in our journey of ambition, offering insights into how to nurture and strengthen these relationships. By examining the role of communication, trust, and mutual support, we can create a strong foundation for our families to thrive.

Effective communication is key to building and maintaining healthy family relationships. This involves being open and honest with our loved ones, listening actively, and expressing our feelings and needs. By fostering a culture of open communication, we can create an environment where everyone feels heard and valued. This chapter offers practical tips for improving communication within our families.

Trust is another essential element of strong family relationships. It is built through consistency, reliability, and mutual respect. By being dependable and showing that we can be counted on, we can strengthen the bonds of trust within our families. This chapter explores the importance of trust and offers strategies for building and maintaining it.

Mutual support is the glue that holds families together. It involves being there for each other through thick and thin, celebrating successes, and offering a shoulder to lean on during difficult times. By fostering a culture of support and encouragement, we can create a strong and resilient family unit. This chapter delves into the importance of mutual support and offers practical tips for nurturing it.

Ultimately, family is the foundation upon which we build our lives. It provides us with a sense of belonging, love, and support that sustains us on our journey of ambition. In this chapter, we celebrate the importance of family and the unique ways in which we can nurture and strengthen these relationships.

6

Chapter 6: Personal Growth

Personal growth is an integral part of the journey of ambition. It involves continuous self-improvement, learning, and development. This chapter explores the importance of personal growth, offering insights into how to cultivate a growth mindset and embrace lifelong learning. By examining the role of self-reflection, goal-setting, and resilience, we can unlock our full potential and achieve our aspirations.

Self-reflection is a crucial aspect of personal growth. It involves taking the time to introspect, evaluate our experiences, and identify areas for improvement. By being honest with ourselves and seeking feedback from others, we can gain valuable insights and make meaningful progress. This chapter offers practical tips for engaging in self-reflection and using it as a tool for growth.

Goal-setting is another essential element of personal growth. It involves identifying our aspirations, setting clear and achievable goals, and creating a plan to achieve them. By staying focused and committed to our goals, we can make steady progress and overcome obstacles. This chapter explores the importance of goal-setting and offers strategies for creating and achieving meaningful goals.

Resilience is the ability to bounce back from setbacks and keep moving forward. It is a crucial quality that enables us to navigate the ups and downs of life with grace and determination. By embracing a growth mindset and viewing challenges as opportunities for learning, we can build resilience and stay committed to our journey of personal growth. This chapter delves into the importance of resilience and offers practical tips for developing it.

Ultimately, personal growth is a lifelong journey that requires continuous effort and commitment. It is about striving to be the best version of ourselves and unlocking our full potential. In this chapter, we celebrate the beauty of personal growth and the unique ways in which we can achieve it.

7

Chapter 7: The Role of Community

Community plays a vital role in our journey of ambition, offering support, inspiration, and a sense of belonging. This chapter explores the importance of community in our personal and professional lives, examining how it shapes our experiences and helps us achieve our goals. By building strong connections and fostering a sense of community, we can create a network of support that sustains us on our journey.

One of the key aspects of community is the sense of belonging it provides. Being part of a community gives us a feeling of connection and shared purpose. This chapter delves into the importance of finding and nurturing communities that align with our values and aspirations. By actively participating in and contributing to these communities, we can create meaningful relationships and a sense of camaraderie.

Support is another crucial element of community. It involves offering and receiving help, encouragement, and guidance. By building a network of supportive individuals, we can navigate the challenges of our journey with greater ease and confidence. This chapter explores the various ways in which communities can offer support, from mentorship and networking opportunities to emotional and practical assistance.

Inspiration is a powerful force that can be found within communities. By surrounding ourselves with individuals who share our passions and aspirations, we can be motivated to push beyond our limits and strive for greatness. This chapter delves into the role of inspiration in our journey of ambition and offers tips for finding and nurturing inspiring communities.

Ultimately, community is an essential part of our journey of ambition. It provides us with a sense of belonging, support, and inspiration that sustains us on our path. In this chapter, we celebrate the importance of community and the unique ways in which it enriches our lives.

8

Chapter 8: Embracing Challenges

Challenges are an inevitable part of the journey of ambition. They test our resilience, push us out of our comfort zones, and help us grow. This chapter explores the importance of embracing challenges and offers strategies for navigating them with grace and determination. By examining the role of mindset, perseverance, and adaptability, we can transform challenges into opportunities for growth and success.

Mindset plays a crucial role in how we perceive and respond to challenges. A growth mindset, which embraces learning and improvement, can help us navigate obstacles with resilience and optimism. This chapter delves into the importance of cultivating a growth mindset and offers practical tips for developing it.

Perseverance is another essential quality that enables us to overcome challenges. It involves staying committed to our goals, even in the face of setbacks and difficulties. By maintaining a strong sense of determination and refusing to give up, we can push through obstacles and achieve our aspirations. This chapter explores the importance of perseverance and offers strategies for staying motivated and focused.

Adaptability is the ability to adjust to changing circumstances and find new solutions to problems. It is a crucial quality that allows us to navigate the unpredictable nature of life with flexibility and resilience. This chapter delves into the importance of being adaptable and offers tips for developing this essential skill.

Ultimately, challenges are an integral part of our journey of ambition. By embracing them with a positive mindset, perseverance, and adaptability, we can transform them into opportunities for growth and success. In this chapter, we celebrate the beauty of challenges and the unique ways in which they shape our journey.

9

Chapter 9: The Power of Purpose

Having a sense of purpose is a driving force that propels us forward on our journey of ambition. It gives our lives meaning and direction, guiding our decisions and actions. This chapter explores the importance of finding and embracing our purpose, offering insights into how to align our ambitions with our deeper values and aspirations. By examining the role of passion, vision, and alignment, we can create a life that is purposeful and fulfilling.

Passion is a powerful force that fuels our ambitions and drives us to achieve our goals. It is the fire that ignites our enthusiasm and keeps us motivated, even in the face of challenges. This chapter delves into the importance of finding and nurturing our passions, and offers tips for staying connected to what truly matters to us.

Vision is the ability to see the bigger picture and envision the future we desire. It provides us with a clear sense of direction and helps us stay focused on our goals. This chapter explores the importance of having a vision and offers strategies for creating and maintaining a compelling vision for our lives.

Alignment is about ensuring that our actions and decisions are in harmony with our values and aspirations. It involves being true to ourselves and making choices that reflect our deeper purpose. This chapter delves into the importance of alignment and offers tips for staying true to our values and purpose.

Ultimately, the power of purpose is a guiding force that shapes our journey of ambition. By finding and embracing our purpose, we can create a life that is meaningful, fulfilling, and aligned with our deepest aspirations. In this chapter, we celebrate the importance of purpose and the unique ways in which it enriches our lives.

10

Chapter 10: Navigating Transitions

Transitions are a natural part of the journey of ambition. Whether it's changing careers, starting a family, or pursuing a new passion, transitions can be both exciting and challenging. This chapter explores the importance of navigating transitions with grace and resilience, offering strategies for embracing change and finding stability in the midst of uncertainty. By examining the role of planning, flexibility, and support, we can navigate transitions with confidence and ease.

Planning is an essential aspect of navigating transitions. It involves setting clear goals, creating a roadmap, and taking proactive steps to prepare for change. By being organized and proactive, we can approach transitions with a sense of clarity and purpose. This chapter offers practical tips for effective planning and preparation.

Flexibility is another crucial quality that helps us navigate transitions. It involves being open to change, adapting to new circumstances, and finding creative solutions to challenges. By embracing flexibility and staying open to new possibilities, we can navigate transitions with resilience and optimism. This chapter delves into the importance of flexibility and offers strategies for developing it.

Support is vital during times of transition. It involves seeking help, guidance, and encouragement from our communities, mentors, and loved ones. By building a strong network of support, we can navigate transitions with greater ease and confidence. This chapter explores the importance of support and offers tips for building and maintaining a supportive network.

Ultimately, transitions are an integral part of our journey of ambition. By navigating them with planning, flexibility, and support, we can embrace change and find stability in the midst of uncertainty. In this chapter, we celebrate the beauty of transitions and the unique ways in which they shape our journey.

11

Chapter 11: Divine Purpose

The concept of divine purpose speaks to the idea that our lives have a higher meaning and are guided by a greater force. This chapter explores the importance of connecting with our divine purpose, offering insights into how spirituality and faith can enrich our journey of ambition. By examining the role of meditation, prayer, and reflection, we can find a deeper sense of meaning and fulfillment in our lives.

Meditation is a powerful practice that helps us connect with our inner selves and the divine. It involves quieting the mind, focusing on the present moment, and cultivating a sense of inner peace. This chapter delves into the importance of meditation and offers practical tips for incorporating it into our daily lives.

Prayer is another essential practice that helps us connect with our divine purpose. It involves communicating with a higher power, seeking guidance, and expressing gratitude. By engaging in regular prayer, we can deepen our spiritual connection and find solace in times of need. This chapter explores the importance of prayer and offers strategies for creating a meaningful prayer practice.

Reflection is the process of introspection and contemplation, allowing us to gain insights and wisdom from our experiences. It involves taking the time to pause, evaluate, and seek meaning in our lives. This chapter delves into the importance of reflection and offers tips for incorporating it into our spiritual journey.

Ultimately, connecting with our divine purpose is a deeply personal and enriching experience. It provides us with a sense of higher meaning and guides our journey of ambition. In this chapter, we celebrate the importance of spirituality and faith and the unique ways in which they enrich our lives.

12

Chapter 12: The Journey Continues

The journey of ambition is a continuous and evolving process. It is marked by growth, learning, and transformation. This chapter explores the importance of staying committed to our journey, embracing the lessons learned, and celebrating our achievements. By examining the role of gratitude, perseverance, and continuous improvement, we can stay motivated and inspired on our path.

Gratitude is a powerful practice that helps us appreciate the progress we have made and the blessings in our lives. It involves acknowledging and expressing thanks for the positive experiences, relationships, and opportunities we encounter. This chapter delves into the importance of gratitude and offers practical tips for cultivating a gratitude practice.

Perseverance is the ability to stay committed to our goals, even in the face of challenges and setbacks. It involves maintaining a strong sense of determination and refusing to give up. By embracing perseverance, we can navigate the ups and downs of our journey with resilience and optimism. This chapter explores the importance of perseverance and offers strategies for staying motivated and focused.

Continuous improvement is the practice of striving to be the best version of ourselves. It involves seeking opportunities for learning and growth, and constantly challenging ourselves to reach new heights. By embracing a mindset of continuous improvement, we can stay inspired and motivated on our journey of ambition. This chapter delves into the importance of continuous improvement and offers tips for cultivating this mindset.

Ultimately, the journey of ambition is a lifelong adventure that requires commitment, resilience, and a sense of purpose. By staying true to ourselves, embracing the lessons learned, and celebrating our achievements, we can create a life that is meaningful and fulfilling. In this final chapter, we celebrate the beauty of the journey and the unique ways in which it continues to unfold.

13

Chapter 13: Mentorship and Guidance

Mentorship is a critical component in the journey of ambition, offering wisdom, support, and a guiding hand. This chapter explores the importance of mentorship, detailing how to find, cultivate, and maintain meaningful mentor relationships. By examining the role of mentors in our personal and professional development, we can unlock valuable insights and accelerate our growth.

Finding the right mentor involves identifying individuals whose experiences and values align with our goals. This chapter delves into the process of seeking out potential mentors and building relationships based on mutual respect and shared aspirations. By being proactive and open to guidance, we can establish connections that provide invaluable support.

Cultivating a strong mentor-mentee relationship requires effort and commitment from both parties. It involves regular communication, active listening, and a willingness to learn and grow together. This chapter offers practical tips for nurturing these relationships and maximizing the benefits of mentorship.

Maintaining mentorship relationships over time is essential for ongoing growth and development. It involves staying connected, expressing gratitude, and continuing to seek guidance and feedback. This chapter explores the importance of long-term mentorship and offers strategies for sustaining these valuable connections.

Ultimately, mentorship is a powerful force that can significantly impact our journey of ambition. By embracing the guidance and wisdom of mentors, we can navigate challenges with greater confidence and achieve our goals. In this chapter, we celebrate the importance of mentorship and the unique ways in which it enriches our lives.

14

Chapter 14: Innovation and Creativity

Innovation and creativity are key drivers of progress and success in our journey of ambition. This chapter explores the importance of thinking outside the box, embracing new ideas, and fostering a culture of creativity. By examining the role of curiosity, experimentation, and risk-taking, we can unlock our creative potential and drive innovation in our personal and professional lives.

Curiosity is the foundation of creativity and innovation. It involves asking questions, seeking new knowledge, and being open to different perspectives. This chapter delves into the importance of cultivating curiosity and offers practical tips for staying curious and engaged.

Experimentation is a crucial aspect of the creative process. It involves trying new approaches, testing hypotheses, and learning from failures. By embracing a mindset of experimentation, we can discover innovative solutions and push the boundaries of what is possible. This chapter explores the importance of experimentation and offers strategies for incorporating it into our daily lives.

Risk-taking is an inherent part of innovation and creativity. It involves stepping out of our comfort zones, embracing uncertainty, and being willing to fail. By taking calculated risks and learning from our experiences, we can drive progress and achieve breakthroughs. This chapter delves into the importance of risk-taking and offers tips for developing the courage to take risks.

Ultimately, innovation and creativity are essential for achieving our ambitions and making a meaningful impact. By fostering a culture of creativity and embracing new ideas, we can drive progress and unlock our full potential. In this chapter, we celebrate the importance of innovation and creativity and the unique ways in which they shape our journey.

15

Chapter 15: Financial Independence

Financial independence is a crucial aspect of the journey of ambition, providing the freedom and security to pursue our goals and dreams. This chapter explores the importance of financial literacy, planning, and management, offering insights into how to achieve and maintain financial independence. By examining the role of budgeting, investing, and debt management, we can create a solid foundation for financial stability and success.

Financial literacy is the knowledge and understanding of financial concepts and practices. It is essential for making informed decisions and managing our finances effectively. This chapter delves into the importance of financial literacy and offers practical tips for improving our financial knowledge and skills.

Budgeting is a key component of financial management. It involves creating a plan for how we will allocate our income and expenses, setting financial goals, and tracking our progress. By staying disciplined and mindful of our spending, we can achieve financial stability and avoid debt. This chapter explores the importance of budgeting and offers strategies for creating and maintaining a budget.

Investing is a powerful tool for building wealth and achieving financial independence. It involves putting our money to work in various assets, such as stocks, bonds, and real estate, to generate returns over time. By making informed investment decisions and diversifying our portfolio, we can grow our wealth and achieve our financial goals. This chapter delves into the importance of investing and offers tips for getting started.

Debt management is another crucial aspect of financial independence. It involves managing and paying off our debts in a responsible and timely manner. By avoiding unnecessary debt and staying on top of our payments, we can achieve financial freedom and reduce stress. This chapter explores the importance of debt management and offers strategies for staying debt-free.

Ultimately, financial independence is essential for achieving our ambitions and living a fulfilling life. By being financially literate, disciplined, and proactive, we can create a solid foundation for success. In this chapter, we celebrate the importance of financial independence and the unique ways in which it empowers us on our journey.

16

Chapter 16: Legacy and Impact

Legacy is about the lasting impact we leave behind and the contributions we make to the world. This chapter explores the importance of creating a meaningful legacy, offering insights into how to make a positive difference in our personal and professional lives. By examining the role of philanthropy, leadership, and mentorship, we can build a legacy that reflects our values and aspirations.

Philanthropy is the act of giving back to society and supporting causes that are important to us. It involves donating our time, resources, and expertise to make a positive impact. This chapter delves into the importance of philanthropy and offers practical tips for finding and supporting meaningful causes.

Leadership is another crucial aspect of building a legacy. It involves inspiring and empowering others to achieve their potential and make a difference. By being a role model and leading by example, we can create a positive ripple effect that extends beyond our immediate sphere of influence. This chapter explores the importance of leadership and offers strategies for becoming an effective and impactful leader.

Mentorship is a powerful way to create a lasting impact. By sharing our knowledge, experiences, and wisdom with others, we can help them achieve their goals and navigate their journeys. This chapter delves into the importance of mentorship and offers tips for becoming a mentor and making a positive difference in the lives of others.

Ultimately, building a legacy is about making a positive impact and leaving the world a better place. By being intentional about our actions and contributions, we can create a legacy that reflects our values and aspirations. In this chapter, we celebrate the importance of legacy and the unique ways in which we can make a difference.

17

Chapter 17: Reflecting and Celebrating

Reflection and celebration are essential parts of the journey of ambition, allowing us to acknowledge our progress, appreciate our achievements, and learn from our experiences. This chapter explores the importance of taking time to reflect and celebrate, offering insights into how to incorporate these practices into our lives. By examining the role of gratitude, self-compassion, and mindfulness, we can stay grounded and motivated on our journey.

Gratitude is the practice of recognizing and appreciating the positive aspects of our lives. It involves acknowledging our blessings, expressing thanks, and cultivating a positive mindset. This chapter delves into the importance of gratitude and offers practical tips for incorporating it into our daily lives.

Self-compassion is the practice of being kind and understanding towards ourselves, especially during times of difficulty and failure. It involves treating ourselves with the same care and compassion that we would offer to a friend. This chapter explores the importance of self-compassion and offers strategies for developing this essential quality.

Mindfulness is the practice of being present and fully engaged in the moment. It involves cultivating awareness of our thoughts, feelings, and experiences without judgment. By practicing mindfulness, we can stay grounded and focused on our journey. This chapter delves into the importance of mindfulness and offers tips for incorporating it into our lives.

Ultimately, reflecting and celebrating are essential for maintaining a sense of balance and perspective on our journey of ambition. By taking time to acknowledge our progress, appreciate our achievements, and learn from our experiences, we can stay motivated and inspired. In this final chapter, we celebrate the importance of reflection and celebration and the unique ways in which they enrich our lives.

The Algorithm of Ambition: A Journey Through Career, Family, and Divine Purpose

In "The Algorithm of Ambition," embark on a transformative journey through the intricate paths of career advancement, family bonds, and the pursuit of a higher purpose. This thought-provoking book delves into the essence of ambition, offering a comprehensive guide to achieving success in all aspects of life.

From the spark of ambition that ignites our dreams to the definition of success that evolves over time, this book explores the multifaceted nature of our aspirations. Discover the importance of resilience and determination as you navigate the twists and turns of your career climb, and learn practical strategies for balancing professional aspirations with personal commitments.

"The Algorithm of Ambition" also highlights the significance of family as the cornerstone of our lives, providing love, support, and a sense of belonging. Gain insights into nurturing healthy family relationships, effective communication, and mutual support, all while embracing personal growth and the power of community.

As you progress through the chapters, you'll uncover the role of creativity, innovation, and financial independence in shaping your journey. Embrace the challenges that come your way and find inspiration in the power of purpose, whether it's through divine guidance, mentorship, or the lasting impact of your legacy.

Reflect on your achievements and celebrate your progress as you continue to evolve and strive for greatness. "The Algorithm of Ambition" is a celebration of the human spirit, offering valuable insights and practical advice to help you unlock your full potential and lead a life that is meaningful,

CHAPTER 17: REFLECTING AND CELEBRATING

fulfilling, and aligned with your deepest aspirations.

Dive into this enriching narrative and let it be your guide as you navigate the complexities of career, family, and divine purpose. Your journey of ambition awaits!

www.ingramcontent.com/pod-product-compliance
Lightning Source LLC
LaVergne TN
LVHW020458080526
838202LV00057B/6023